Love Your Books
by Angie Rowe

ILLUSTRATED BY
Natalia Rowe

DESIGNED BY
Dan Clarke - Telford Repro

"For all the people who dedicate their time helping animals to live a wonderful life"

Angela Rowe
angie.rowe@loveyour-books.com

www.loveyour-books.com

Love Your Dog

Content Copyright © Angela Rowe
                    Protect My Work 2018
Illustration Copyright © Natalia Rowe
                    Protect My Work 2018

ISBN 978-1-9163572-0-4

Love Your Books

by Angie Rowe

Love your Cat

Love your Hamster

Love your Rabbit

Love your Budgie

Love your Horse

Love your Fish

To Parents, Carers & Teachers

These 'Love Your' Books are to help bring out empathy, compassion and kindness within your child and their natural loving nature to shine through.

To love all animals domestic and wild, whether big or small is one of the best traits to have.

Cruelty should **NEVER** belong in a childs heart.

Your Dog needs water

Your Dog needs walks

Without walks

Your Dog needs affection

Your Dog needs toys

Without toys

DON'T

- **HIT YOUR DOG**

- **SHOUT AT YOUR DOG**

- **GET ANGRY AT YOUR DOG**

- **IGNORE YOUR DOG**

- **LEAVE YOUR DOG OUTSIDE IN HOT OR COLD WEATHER**

IT IS CRUEL

DO

- BE KIND TO YOUR DOG

- BE AFFECTIONATE TO YOUR DOG

- BE RESPONSIBLE FOR YOUR DOG

REMEMBER
YOUR DOG LOVES
YOU VERY MUCH

LOVE YOUR
DOG
WITH ALL YOUR
HEART

In a world
where you can
be anything
BE KIND

Colour me correctly

Colour me
CRAZY

Printed in Great Britain
by Amazon